Юлий Даниэль

ТЮРЕМНЫЕ СТИХИ

Дж. Филип О'Гара, Инк.
Чикаго

PRISON POEMS

by
Yuli Daniel

Translated by
David Burg and Arthur Boyars

○

J. Philip O'Hara, Inc.
Chicago

Library of Congress Cataloging in Publication Data

Daniel', IUlii Markovich, 1925–
    Prison poems.

    Add t.p. in Russian; text in English and Russian.

    I. Title.
PG3479.6.A46T5   1972   891.7'1'44   76-186888
ISBN 0-87955-501-7

J. Philip O'Hara, Inc. 20 East Huron, Chicago, 60611

First Printing E

CONTENTS

YULI DANIEL AND HIS POETRY

The last classic Russian poet, Anna Akhmatova, described Yuli Daniel as "a poet with a great and clear mind" and Daniel has always thought of himself as above all a poet. Yet his poetry has remained largely unpublished. It was his prose, which appeared in the West under the pseudonym "Nikolai Arzhak", that earned Daniel five years jail in February, 1966.

The way he conducted himself during his trial - defending his work, his ideals and his friend and co-defendant, Andrei Sinyavski - made him almost a household name throughout the world. This is not the place to recapitulate the notorious events of the Sinyavski-Daniel trial,[1] nor to give an appreciation of Daniel's stinging, yet humane, satires that led to it. But I should like to sketch in some little known background on Daniel as a man and as a poet - drawn partly from my personal knowledge of him.

Daniel's "Prison Poems" which appear in this volume are a product of "samizdat", the clandestine cottage industry which typewritten publishing has become in Russia. This book is the first collection of Daniel's poetry and it is also the first time his poetry has appeared in the original Russian. I should like to make it absolutely clear that I am solely responsible for the decision to publish "Prison Poems" - Daniel had nothing to do with this decision or with the dispatch of his work abroad.

In 1924 a young Russian-Jewish revolutionary, Mordecai Meyerovich, published an epic novel on which he had been working since his return from the Civil War. Written in Yiddish, it described his life and the tragic events that took place in his small

Jewish town in the depths of the Byelorussian "Pale",
(the area where Jews were officially allowed to
settle) when it became a battlefield during the First
World War. Mordecai's own hard apprenticeship as
a tailor at the age of 11, his first contact with the
revolutionaries, the sudden eruption of the war with
its pogroms and the subsequent deportations of
Jews to the Urals - indeed the whole life of the Pale
in those terrible years of trouble - are all contained
in At A Time Like This. The Soviet Literary
Encyclopaedia wrote, six years later, that this first
novel immediately put its author "in the forefront of
Soviet Jewish prosewriters". The book[2] appeared
under the pseudonym "Mark Daniel" and Meyerovich
later adopted this "nom de succès" as his civil name.

More novels and short stories in Yiddish followed.
Most of them were promptly translated into Russian.
The plays were performed all over the Soviet Union.
Mark Daniel's work enjoyed a good deal of popular
success, as well as receiving official approval. For
invariably his hero was the self-sacrificing
revolutionary - worker, artist, commissar. His last
play was published in the year of the Great Purge,
1937. Then he fell silent and died of tuberculosis in
December 1940. He was just over 40.

Mark Daniel was an artist who strove in his work
to be faithful to his own vision of life. He was also a
man of conscience: he felt those social and national
injustices, which he knew so well from the days of the
old Empire, as if they were a personal injury. His
ideals as an artist and a man led him into the
Revolution. A quarter of a century after his death,
Mark's son, Yuli, proclaimed them again in his work
and at his trial. He remained faithful to them even
though the State, which his father helped to create -
first with his gun then with his pen - has since come
to feel that true art and justice threaten the supremacy

of the established order.

Mark Daniel's only son was born in 1925. He named him Yuli after a heroic commissar he had known in Minsk during the Civil War. (This man's self-sacrifice and purity impressed the senior Daniel so greatly that a few years later he was to write the most successful play of his career about him. It was entitled <u>Yulis, or the Four Days</u> and it was staged in 1931 by, among others, Samuel Mikhoels, one of the greatest actors and directors in post-revolutionary Russia.)

In spite of Mark Daniel's literary success, life was not easy for the Daniels during Yuli's childhood. The 1930s were a time of acute shortages and sometimes of outright famine in Russia, and the enormous fees for state-approved art, as they exist today, had not yet been introduced. The family lived in the centre of Moscow in one small odd-shaped room in Maroseika Street. (A room that used to be part of a rotunda in an Empire house: it still looked like a chunk of curved passage abruptly cut off on both sides by unexpected walls.) The famine did not affect the Daniels directly, but the moral issues arising from it, as well as from the growing "Stalinization" of Russian life in general, were felt more by them than by most other families. Most Russians in those grim times were concerned only with sheer physical survival. But to the Daniels the Revolution was like their own child, not much less so than their son. (Yuli's mother, Manya, together with her first husband, took part in the Civil War in her own right.) No parent can look on calmly as his son takes to crime. And the Daniels could not remain indifferent as they watched their Revolution turn delinquent.

Yuli was growing up in an atmosphere of agonized devotion to the Revolution and of baffled pain at the levelling down of all the arts which was imposed with such ruthlessness in the 1930s. Later in life he made his parents' concerns his own. But unlike today's sceptical, and often cynical, Russian teenagers, Yuli and his generation, when they were adolescents, managed to combine a curious purity of thought and feeling with an uncomplicated, romantic acceptance of official causes, such as the Spanish Civil War, and the worship of Stalin. Although they saw the cruelties of the regime and often suffered from them directly, they somehow managed to regard them as incidental.[3] In poetry, rhetoric moved them more than lyricism. Apart from Mayakovski, Eduard Bagritsky was the most passionately sincere of all revolutionary rhetoricians and he was also a great master of evocative poetic description. Yuli began to write verse before he was ten and Bagritsky soon became his first and most lasting love in poetry. His energetic defiance still echoes in such poems in this collection as "The New Year March" or "In the Ring"; Bagritsky himself could almost have written "A House" with its transformation of the banal into a thing to be marvelled at for the first time ever.

History did not afford Yuli much time for peaceful poetic and intellectual development. The war between Germany and Russia began when he was sixteen. He went from his school desk almost directly into the trenches when he was eighteen and before he was twenty he was already a war invalid drawing a pension. I am not sure whether he was hit directly in the lungs, but in any case his very serious wound affected them permanently. (This made his later stay in the old Vladimir prison with its cold stone walls a very nearly murderous experience for him.)

By 1946 Daniel recovered sufficiently to continue his education. He studied Russian literature first in

Kharkov, then in Moscow, graduated in 1951 and then taught literature in school for six years. The school approach to literature was particularly arid at that time. To what extent such and such work was a harbinger of the glorious present, and how it "unmasked" the social iniquities of the pre-Revolutionary past - these were the main questions asked. Daniel went far beyond them in his teaching and this brought trouble with the education authorities. Perhaps it was the harassment that made him abandon his career in the late 1950s, or perhaps it was the realization that he could support his wife and his young son by practising his true vocation - writing poetry.

Throughout the post-war years Daniel continued to compose verse steadily. (He began to write prose in 1952 but had only worked on it systematically since 1957.) By the mid 1950s he developed an amazing facility for versification and he put this skill to a money-making pursuit. A good deal of poetry gets translated in the Soviet Union, particularly from the hundred or so languages of various Soviet nationalities into Russian; the Communist Party is anxious to encourage and spread "national culture which is socialist in content". From 1957 until his arrest in 1965 Daniel became one of the foremost poetic translators in the country. He published scores of translations from languages such as Ukrainian, Armenian, Balkar or Yiddish. All were competent professional jobs and some much more than that - the rendering of the powerful surrealist poetry of the Ukrainian Ivan Drach, for instance. There are few good translators of poetry, and since the demand is great the work is relatively well paid - well enough to allow Daniel, and many other poets like him, to support their families and to have sufficient time left for their own more personal writing.

11

Daniel's poetry was constantly gaining in depth
and skill. From Boris Pasternak he learned the art
of juxtaposing the strikingly unusual with the starkly
simple and the way of using evocative sounds and
quickly-changing rhythms (see "February"). He also
assimilated his sense of exhilaration, almost
breathless freedom. Nikolai Zabolotsky, the doyen
of Russian surrealism, taught him the power of poetic
meditation. He absorbed the rhythms of classical
Russian folksongs with their passionate plaintiveness
("Another Song") and of modern concentration camp
folklore with its dashing abandon, despair, expressive
vulgarity and cocky defiance ("1965", "About These
Poems"). The cadence of Jewish wit was part of his
family heritage ("A Prayer"), and one of his great
mentors was Heinrich Heine, with his very Jewish
sense of satire.

By 1965 Daniel was developing into a mature poet
and what he produced was very much better than the
majority of what was being regularly published in
Russia - though to keep things in perspective, one
must admit he had not reached the heights of the best
work of his mentors. On the other hand, he was in no
way inhibited about being a poet. He was always
pleased to read his work aloud to friends when they
asked him, and his lightness of touch when reading
reflected his dislike of those grand postures which so
often mar the work of even the best Russian poets.
Unlike many other unpublished Soviet writers, Daniel
did not until recently distribute his work in typescript.
He was always mindful of his alter ego in the West and
was careful not to attract the attention of the secret
police. Although his verse was by no means all
political and much of it could be easily printed,
that he never published anything, nor took part in
any official readings, was for reasons that had more
to do with politics than with poetry. His lyrical verse

was easily publishable, but his mature grasp of
past events would not allow him to be dispensed
in strictly non-lethal doses.[4]

The post-war arrests and persecutions, the
denunciation of Stalin in 1956 and the beginnings of a
true intellectual debate within Soviet society had a
deep effect on Daniel's earlier, somewhat idyllic,
view of the Russian social order. The official anti-
Semitism, as it emerged in the late 1940s, and the
destruction of Yiddish culture, were a profound
shock to him. Unlike his father, Daniel was a Russian,
not a Jewish writer, having completely assimilated
Russian culture, attitudes and ways of thinking. The
small Jewish town of his father's youth, with its
ancient customs and its timeless religious beliefs,
was almost as remote from his generation as the
medieval ghetto (though I believe that unlike most of
his contemporaries of similar cultural background,
Daniel does know Yiddish).

The "anti-cosmopolitan" campaign of 1948-53, when
people in Daniel's position were subjected to
discrimination in jobs and education, had to bear
insults, were threatened with deportation, affected
them even more deeply than the worst pogrom had
shaken their fathers or grandfathers. For before the
Revolution Jews at least knew where they stood: they
suffered because they insisted on being different. And
their suffering had a deep meaning for them. But
Daniel's generation identified with Russia. Their
Jewishness did not matter all that much to them, and
when they too were rejected, it was a meaningless,
gratuitous agony.

Stalinist persecution affected most Jews, though
naturally in different ways - depending on whether they
thought of themselves as assimilated or Jewish Jews.
But, untypically, Yuli had to bear the brunt of both
kinds of persecution. He had close personal connections

13

through his father with the world of specifically
Jewish culture. This was completely destroyed in
Stalin's last years and on the 12th August 1952,
twenty-six Yiddish writers were shot on a charge of
wanting to detach the Crimea from the Soviet Union
and to set up a Jewish state there. Some of those
executed had been friends of Yuli's father. All
Yiddish literature was banned, including Mark
Daniel's work, many confiscated books were stored
in a half-flooded cellar in Moscow. Yuli found out
about this and tried to salvage some of them. He
succeeded, but the cold water in the cellar was too
much for his weak lungs and he came down with
severe and protracted pneumonia.

The nightmare that he and his friends had lived
through had a profound effect on Yuli Daniel's work.
Yet none of his blunter poems could pass the
censorship and he did not want to be known merely as
an author of lyrical verse. This probably led to the
last act of his drama as a writer - the decision to
concentrate on prose, to publish it abroad under a
secret pseudonym, and to face the consequences if he
were found out.

"Prison Poems" are partly a reflection on these
consequences, partly a statement of what it means to
be a prisoner in a Soviet security police (KGB) gaol.
The first poem was written approximately a month
after Daniel's arrest, the last after the sentencing a
few days before deportation to a forced labour camp.
With his usual transparent honesty and simplicity,
Daniel registered the whole range of his emotions as
he was being grilled by the KGB - his despair and
longing for those he loves, his loyalty to his friends
and fears that his loyalty to his country might be
doubted, his sarcastic contempt for his jailers. He
felt great guilt at "failing to spare another's heart",
dragging those near to him into his ordeal, and this

was his lowest moment. His highest was reached
when he realised at the trial that he was no longer
just another Russian prisoner: that he had become -
by an act of Fate, as he saw it - a symbol, a man of
destiny speaking for those "who died mute deaths".

The poems themselves are quite explicit and need
no interpretation. I should only like to add that in the
six years since they were written, Daniel has more
than lived up to the moral burden which he accepted
with such great and unforced pathos in "The Sentence".
In the book My Testimony his erstwhile co-prisoner,
Anatoli Marchenko, tells us how Daniel rejected all
privilege, repentance and submission on arrival in
the camp. In fact he insisted on doing the same back-
breaking manual labour as all prisoners. His wife
(now exiled herself for protesting against the invasion
of Czechoslovakia) related how he was tortured for
this - by hunger, by cold, even by exposing him to
mosquitoes in the Mordvinian swamps where he
had been sent to serve his sentence. Several times
he went on prolonged hunger strikes to protest against
the conditions of imprisonment. The last time was in
June 1969 when he demanded with other prisoners
that Alexander Ginsburg, who joined him in the camps
for compiling the White Book on his case, should be
allowed officially to marry the woman who was in fact
his wife and that she should then be allowed to visit
him. This action succeeded, but on the 11th July 1969,
the "troublemaker" Daniel was transferred to the
Vladimir prison - the hungriest, the coldest, the
most desperate and debilitating jail in Russia. He
spent fourteen months there and was released on 12th
September 1970, five years to the day after his arrest.
The authorities did not permit his return to Moscow.
This restriction was illegal even in terms of Soviet
law (his original sentence did not include exile from
domicile), but for once Daniel accepted it. "I'm tired,

tired", this was his first public statement on leaving jail.

Daniel now works as a petty clerk. He again translates poetry and writes his own. He was even allowed to publish a few translations in a provincial literary magazine. He lives in Kaluga, a small town some 90 miles from the capital. The town itself is not particularly beautiful, but its surrounding landscapes have been much loved by several generations of Russian writers and painters who glorified them as the gentle heartland of the country which was so brutal to so many of them.

One day the Sinyavski-Daniel trial may be recognized as a turning point in Russian history. The protest of an important section of Russian history. The protest of an important section of Russian intelligentsia against state-sanctioned lawlessness certainly dates back to it and was largely centred around it for a long time. But even the most dramatic flowering of democracy in Russia will not make good the suffering inflicted on the author of these poems. Only Daniel himself might perhaps then consider it to have been worthwhile.

David Burg
London, June 1971

Notes

1. The Sinyavski-Daniel case has been fully
documented in Alexander Ginsburg's White Book
(published in Russian in Frankfurt in 1967).
White Book is unavailable in English, but much of
its material is reproduced in On Trial, a
collection of documents edited by Leopold Labedz
and Max Hayward, Collins and Harvill Press, 1967.
This collection includes more western material
than Ginsburg's original but omits some important
Russian documents.

2. In a zait aza (At a Time Like This), Shtrom,
Moscow, 1924.

3. For the best statement of their attitudes, see
Nina Kosterina's "Diary", Novy Mir, No. 12,
1962.

4. Many younger writers refuse to accept the division
of their work into the publishable and unpublishable.
I was reliably told that when Joseph Brodsky
returned from his much-publicized exile in 1966,
Yevtushenko arranged for a selection of his poetry
to be published in the magazine Yunost
(circulation 2,000,000). But when the censorship
killed some of his poems, he withdrew the rest,
thus declining a lucrative and spectacular, but
relatively innocuous, official debut.

I should like to express my gratitude to Mr. Joseph
Berger (Ytzhak Barzilai) for some of the information
in this introduction. D.B.

PRISON POEMS
ТЮРЕМНЫЕ СТИХИ

Вспоминайте меня, я вам всем по строке
    подарю.
Не тревожьте себя, я долги заплачу к
    январю.
Я не буду хитрить и скулить, о прощеньи
    моля,
Это зрелость пришла, и пора оплатить
    векселя.

Непутевый, хмельной, захлебнувшийся
    плотью земной,
Я трепался и врал, чтобы вы оставались
    со мной.
Как я мало дарил. И как много я принял
    даров
Под неверный, под зыбкий, под мой
    рассыпавшийся кров.

Я словами умел и убить, и влюбить
    наповал.
И, теряя прицел, я себя самого убивал.
Но благая судьба сочинила счастливый
    конец,
Я достоен теперь ваших мыслей и ваших
    сердец.

И меня к вам влечет, как бумагу влечет
    к янтарю.
Вспоминайте меня: я вам всем по строке
    подарю.
По неловкой, по горькой, тоскою
    пропахшей строке,
Чтоб любили меня, когда буду от вас
    вдалеке.

19.10.65

Commit me to your memories, I'll give you each a
    verse.
Don't be alarmed, I'll pay my debts by January.
I won't use tricks or whine and beg for mercy.
I've ripened and it's time to pay my debts.

Unbridled drunkard, gorging myself on carnal joys,
I chattered on and lied to keep you with me.
I gave so little! But I took so much
Into my dilapidated, tottering house.

Once I could kill outright with words, also seduce,
And, having lost my aim, I turned death on myself.
But good fortune brought about the happy ending,
Now I am worthy of your thoughts and hearts.

I'm drawn to you as paper is to amber.
Commit me to your memories, I'll give you each a
    verse.
A verse for each of you, clumsy, bitter and anguished,
To make you love me when I'm far away.

19th October 1965

СТИХИ С ЭПИГРАФОМ

А зачем вам карандаш?
Писать стихи.
Какие стихи?
Не беспокойтесь, лирику.
Про любовь?
Может, и про любовь.

Да, про любовь, наперекор "глазку",
Что день и ночь таращится из двери.
Да, про любовь — про ревность, про тоску.
Про поиски, свершенья и потери.

Да, про любовь —среди казенных стен,
Зеленых, с отраженным желтым светом,
Да, про нее, до исступления, с тем,
Чтоб никогда не забывать об этом:

О дрожи душ, благоговеньи тел,
О причащеньи счастью и утрате,
Я про любовь всю жизнь писать хотел
И лишь теперь коснулся благодати.

Да, про нее. Всему наперекор,
Писать про суть, сдирая позолоту;
Им кажется, что взяли на прикол,
А я к тебе, — сквозь стены, прямиком,
Мне до тебя одна секунда лету.

Мне все твердят: "Молчи, забудь, учись
Смирению, любовник обнищавший."
А я целую клавиши ключиц
И слушаю аккорды обещаний.

A POEM WITH AN EPIGRAPH

Why do you need the pencil?
To write verse.
What sort of verse?
Don't worry, it's only lyric poetry.
Is it about love?
Perhaps it will be.

Yes, it is love, so as to defy the peephole
That watches from the door all day and night.
Yes, it is love - jealousy and anguish,
Searching, acquiring, losing.

Yes, it is love, behind official walls,
With yellow light reflected in their green,
It is the theme, and in a state of frenzy
So as never to forget these things:

Quivering souls, bodies all devout,
Communion with joy and then bereavement,
I wanted all my life to write of love,
But only now have I become inspired.

It is the theme! And so, defiantly
I'd write about the essence and strip off the gilt;
They think I'm anchored here, once and for all,
But I'll make straight for you, right through the walls,
One second's flying and I'll reach you.

"Keep quiet, forget it," they've all been telling me.
"Learn to be humble, you beggar of a lover!"
While I kiss the keyboard of your clavicles
And hear the harmonies of promises.

23

Я твой, я твой, до сердцевины весь,
И я готов года и версты мерить.
Я жду тебя. Ну, где же как не здесь,
Тебя любить и, что любим, поверить.

19.10.65

I'm yours, yours to the core, yours entirely,
And I'm ready to start marking off the years and
    miles.
I'm waiting for you. Where, if not here,
Shall I love you believing I am loved.

19th October 1965

ДОМ

В окно я глянул и увидел дом.
Обычный дом — немыслимое чудо:
Он был семи- или восьмиэтажный,
И в первом этаже был магазин,
И выше были окна без решеток,
И каждое окно освещено
Своим особым светом, непохожим
На свет соседних. Это оттого,
Что там на окнах были занавески
И были шторы — словом — было то,
Чем люди загораживаться вправе
От посторонних взглядов. Я, однако,
Сумел глазами памяти увидеть,
Узнать лицо потерянного рая:
Там были стулья и цветы на окнах,
Когда-то презиравшиеся мною,
Цветы в горшках, зеленые богини,
С которых пыль стирают по субботам.
Там лампы в потолки не уходили,
Не прятались за мутным плексигласом,
Висели в кринолинах абажуров,
Собой венчали шаткие торшеры,
Со стен свисали ..Там на книжных полках
Лежали неожиданные вещи:
Шнурки от туфель, биллиардный шарик,
Чулок с иголкой в штопке, позабытой,
Из-за гостей, нагрянувших врасплох;
Еще рецепт — его уже с неделю
Никто никак не может отыскать...
Там были скатерти, на них ножи и вилки —
Орава режущих и колющих предметов ..
Там, в этом доме, было много женщин —
Не медсестер и не стенографисток,
А просто женщин. В платьицах домашних.

A HOUSE

I looked through the window and I saw a house.
An ordinary house, a miracle beyond belief.
It stood seven or eight floors high,
The ground floor was a shop,
And the windows above it had no bars,
And every window was lit up
With a special kind of light, quite different
From the light of those adjoining it. And this because
The windows possessed curtains
And blinds, in short, the means
Which people have the right to use against
The stares of strangers. But I
Could see the face of a lost paradise
With eyes of memory and I recognized it.
Chairs there were and flowers on the window sills,
Which once aroused my scorn,
Potted plants, the green Goddesses,
To be dusted every Saturday;
There the electric bulbs were not embedded in the ceilings.
Nor did they hide behind dim strips of plastic,
But hung inside the shades of crinoline,
Or crowned the wobbling standard lamps,
Or dangled from the walls... Unusual things
Lay on the bookshelves: such as
A shoe-lace, a billiard ball,
A stocking ready with its darning needle, forgotten
Since the arrival of unexpected guests;
Also a prescription - hunted high and low
For what, by now, has almost been a week;
There were tablecloths laid out with knives and forks,
A throng of sharp and pointed articles...
In that house there were many women,
And they were neither nurses nor shorthand typists,
But simply women. In everyday attire.

Они, сколовши волосы небрежно
И рукава по локоть засучив,
Купали в новых ванночках младенцев,
Со лба к затылку отгоняя воду,
Чтоб мыльной пене в глазки не попасть.
И отблеск розовых мелькающих локтей
Являлся сполохом на сердце, обещая
Округлое и теплое свершенье
Потом, когда погаснет в доме свет ...
Да, я забыл сказать, что по фасаду
На доме было множество балконов,
Где стыли на ветру велосипеды,
И в сети гамаков шли косяками
Проворные снежинки ... Дом трещал —
Его неудержимо распирало,
Давило изнутри избытком жизни.
В нем жило все — от шпильки головной,
От кошки и собаки — до нескладных
Подростков с неуклюжими руками,
Украдкой сочиняющих стихи.
И алые частицы этой жизни
Сквозь кладку стен, как запах, проходили.
Летели сквозь зашторенные окна
Ко мне, ко мне, к откинутой фрамуге
Окна, перед которым я стоял,
На стол взобравшись. Целых полминуты
Я прикасался к человечьей жизни.
Потом я спрыгнул на пол. Вот и все.
... Я знаю, что неловки эти строки,
Что мой товарищ глянет неподкупно,
Серьезно покачает головой
И скажет мне:"А что, как эта проза,
Да и плохая?" "Да — скажу я — да.
Плохая. Проза. Хуже не бывает..."

6.I0.65

Hair casually pinned back,
Their sleeves rolled up to the elbow,
They bathed their babies in brand-new baby baths,
Smoothing the water from their foreheads to their crowns
To keep the soap out of their tiny eyes.
The glow of their pink flashing elbows
Seemed like lightning kindled in the heart. It promised
Fulfilment, round and warm,
Later when all the house's lights were out...
Oh yes, I forgot to tell you, that the front wall
Supported many balconies
Where bicycles stood freezing in the wind
And swirling shoals of snowflakes poured into
The nets of hammocks... The house was cracking open!
It just could not contain
The excess pressure of the life within it!
It was all alive - from a hairpin,
A dog, a cat, to gawky adolescents
With their clumsy fingers
Who wrote their poems stealthily.
The scarlet molecules of this life
Suffused the very brickwork of the walls just like an odour;
They were flying through the curtains on the windows
To me, towards me who, having climbed onto the table,
    now stood before
A window's open frame. For all of half a minute
I shared in human life.
Then I jumped down. That was all.
...I know these lines are awkward,
That a friend of mine will fix me with his incorruptible gaze,
Will earnestly shake his head
And say to me: "Could this be merely prose?
And bad prose too?" "Yes," I'll reply, "of course.
It is bad prose. The very worst there is..."

6th October 1965

Околеваю от тоски:
Одолеваю я "Бруски".

2.II.65

Flattened by boredom
Under a load of "Whetstones".

2nd November 1965

СОРОКАЛЕТИЕ

Как славно знать, что был ты несерьезен,
Что ты плевал на важные дела
И что беспечность, как смола из сосен
Свободно и естественно текла.

Пусть рот кривят солидные мужчины
С высот сорокалетья своего.
Как славно знать, что не было причины
И что тебя кружило озорство.

О тени предков, преданных идеям,
Сюжетцы для возвышенных стихов.
Куда как лучше стать себе злодеем
За просто так, во имя пустяков.

Брести без брода   и ваять из снега,
Уйти в бега,   влюбиться на пари ...
Мальчишество мое, мой **alter ego**
Со мной всегда на равных говори.

Никто не властен над своей планидой,
Но можно ей подножку дать, шаля ...
Эй, навер**ху**! За простоту не выдай.
Не расступайся, мать сыра земля.

12.II.65

MY FORTIETH BIRTHDAY

It's nice to know one's not been serious
And never gave a damn for vital business,
That life has flowed along lightheartedly
Like resin from a pine, free as in nature.

Let reputable men screw up their lips
Perched on the pinnacle of their forty years.
It's nice to know you've acted crazily
And accidents have spun you round and round.

O ghosts of ancestors, devoted to ideas,
Poor subjects for some lofty lines of verse!
Far better just to become a scoundrel
Without a reason, all in the name of folly.

Better to flounder out of one's depth, carve out of snow,
Run and keep on running, or fall in love for a bet...
My boyhood, my alter ego,
Please, let's always talk on equal terms.

No one controls his fate, that's written in the stars,
But you can stick your feet out tripping her,
    perversely...
Hey, you up there! Don't give me away just for being
    half-witted!
Don't gape under my feet, good Mother Earth.

                                    12th November 1965

33

ПЕСЕНКА

За неделею неделя
Тает в дыме сигарет.
В этом странном заведеньи
Все как будто сон и бред.

Птицы бродят по карнизам,
И в замках поют ключи.
Нереальный мир пронизан
Грубым запахом мочи.

Тут не гаснет свет ночами,
Тут не ярок свет дневной,
Тут молчанье, как начальник,
Утвердилось надо мной.

Задыхайся от безделья,
Колотись об стенку лбом —
За неделю неделя
Тает в дыме голубом.

Тут без устали считают,
Много ли осталось дней.
Тут, безумствуя, мечтают
Все о ней, о ней, о ней.

Тут стучат шаги конвоя —
Или это сердца стук?
Тут не знаешь, как на воле,
Кто твой враг и кто твой друг.

AN AIR

Week after week
Dissolves in smoke from cigarettes
In this curious establishment
Everything's dream or else delirium.

Birds stray along the ledges,
Keys sing in the locks.
The world of unreality is steeped
In urine's pungent smell.

In here the light doesn't go off at night,
In here the light isn't too strong by day.
In here silence, the managing director,
Has taken me over.

You can choke with nothing to do,
Or beat your head against the wall,
Week after week
Dissolves in blue smoke.

Tirelessly, you're counting here
How many days are still to go.
Here in your frenzied fantasy you dream
Of her, of her, always of her.

In here the thump of the warders' steps -
Or is it the thumping of your heart?
In here you don't know as you would outside
Who's your friend and who's your foe.

Это злое сновиденье,
Пустота меж да и нет.
За неделею неделя
Тает в дыме сигарет.

Тает в дыме ...

9.II.65

This evil terrifying dream,
Limbo between "yes" and "no",
Week after week
Dissolves in smoke from cigarettes.

Dissolves in smoke...

9th November 1965

ПЕСНЯ

"На беленьком камушке сидючи"

Что-то скучно мне без воли,
Что-то дни идут впустую,
Сочинить бы песню что ли,
Немудреную, простую.

Сочинить про то, что снится,
Прикоснуться, как руками, -
Про бегущую водицу,
Да про бел-горючий камень.

Как на камешке сидела,
Воду в горсти наливала,
На три стороны глядела,
Напевала, колдовала:

Глянет влево - словно рядом
Бубны бьют, поют колеса,
И цыганка темным взглядом
В сердце мне глядит раскосо.

Глянет вправо - обернется
Королевишной далекой
А кому под стать бороться
С белорукой, синеокой?

Как на камушке сидела,
По воде ладонью била,
На три стороны глядела,
Про четвертую забыла.

A SONG

"As I was sitting on a white rock"
[A Russian folksong]

I feel bored without my freedom, I don't know why.
The days pass without purpose, I don't know why.
It would be nice to write a song,
Simple and uninvolved.

To write a song about my dreams,
Almost to touch them with my hands;
Write about the water flowing round
A white rock in its stream.

How she sat on that white rock,
Cupped the water in her hands,
Looked around on three sides
While she sang her witch's song.

When she looked to the left I seemed to hear
The noise of tambourines, the grind of wheels;
And a gipsy with her slanting eyes
Looked deep and straight into my heart.

When she looked to the right she was transformed
Into a faraway princess out of a fairy tale;
And who could resist this one,
Fair-haired and blue-eyed?

She sat on that white rock
Hitting the water with her hand;
Looked around her on three sides
But forgot about the fourth.

39

Обернись ко мне собою,
Обернись ко мне самою,
Обернись ко мне судьбою —
Я тоску свою омою.

   Маяту и опасенья
   Поцелуями уйму я,
   Нам обоим во спасение
   С камушка тебя сниму я.

5.12.65

Turn towards me with your face,
Turn towards me with your soul,
Turn towards me and be my fate -
And I'll wash away my pain.

    Anxiety and grief will fade
    Confronted by my kisses,
    And so that we can both be saved
    I'll lift you off the rock.

5th December 1965

ДРУЗЬЯМ

Была щедра не в меру божья милость ,
Я был богат. Не проходило дня,
Чтоб манною небесной не валилось
Сочувствие людское на меня.

    Я подставлял изнеженные горсти,
    Я усмехался: "Господу хвала."-
    Когда входили караваном гости
    С бесценным грузом света и тепла.

Но только здесь сумел уразуметь я
От ваших рук, от ваших глаз вдали,
Что в страшное ненастное трехлетье
Лишь вы меня от гибели спасли.

    Нет, не единым хлебом люди живы.
    Вы помогли мне выиграть бои,
    Вы кровь и жизнь в мои вливали жилы -
    О лекари, о доноры мои.

Все кончено. Сейчас мне очень плохо.
Кружится надо мною непокой.
Кому вздохнуть: "Моя ты суматоха..."
И лба коснуться теплою рукой ?

    Все кончено. Нескоро воля будет,
    Да и надежда теплится едва.
    Но в тишине опустошенных буден
    Вы превратились в звуки и слова.

Вы, светлые, в тюремные тетради
Вошли, пройдя подспудные пути.
Всех во плоти я должен был утратить,
Чтоб в ритмах и созвучьях обрести.

TO MY FRIENDS

God's grace has surely been over-abundant.
Riches were mine. Hardly a day would pass
When human sympathy did not alight on me
Like manna from the sky.

    I cupped my slender fingers to receive it
    Ironically smiling: "God be praised,"
    As a whole caravan of guests descended
    Bearing its priceless freight of light and warmth.

Now, far from your hands, far from your eyes,
It's only now I've really understood
That it was you who saved me from destruction
In those dark and terrible three years.

    No, man does not live by bread alone!
    It was your help made me win the battles.
    You poured blood and life back into my veins,
    O you who revived me, you who gave me your blood!

It's finished. I'm in trouble up to my neck.
Anxiety is circling around me.
But is there a soul to sigh and say: "You old trouble-
    maker..."
And stroke my forehead with a warming hand?

    It's finished. It'll be a long time before I'm out.
    Even the ray of hope now hardly glimmers.
    But in the silences of ravaged days
    You've been transfigured into sounds and words.

You've settled on these prison written pages,
Travelled uncharted roads of darkness, though drenched
    in light.
As flesh and blood I had to lose you all
To rediscover you in metre and in rhyme.

Вы здесь, со мной, вседневно, ежечасно,
Прощеньем, отпущением грехов:
Ведь в мире все покорно и подвластно
Божественной невнятице стихов ...

6.12.65

You stand beside me here, each day and every
    hour,
You are my pardon and my absolution:
For everything in this world bows and subjects
    itself
To the divine confusion of the poem...

6th December 1965

ЕЩЕ ОДНА ПЕСЕНКА

То ли быль, то ли небыль
Из веселого сна?
Я в сражениях не был
И не пил я вина.

Не был пулею мечен
И стихов не писал,
Не глядел я на женщин
Не любил, не бросал;

Не смеялся, не плакал,
Дни за днями губя,
И не ставил я на кон
Ни других, ни себя;

Не плясал неуклюже,
На ветру не дрожал,
В подмосковные стужи
По лыжне не бежал.

С красотой не венчался
И друзей не имел,
На волнах не качался,
Песни петь не умел.

И в осеннюю сырость
Не плутал по земле –
Это все мне приснилось
В зарешеченной мгле.

12.12.65

ANOTHER SONG

Is it fact or is it fiction,
Part of an entertaining dream?
I never went off to battles
And I never drank wine.

    I wasn't scarred by a bullet
    And I didn't write verse.
    I never looked at women,
    Didn't love them or leave them.

I didn't laugh, didn't cry
Wasting day after day,
Never risked others or myself
On the turn of a card.

    I never danced in my clumsy fashion,
    Never quivered in the wind,
    Never shot by on a ski track
    Near Moscow on a frosty day.

I was not married to beauty
And I had no friends,
The waves never rolled me over
And I couldn't sing songs.

    I never roamed aimlessly
    On a wet autumn day -
    I dreamed all of this
    In the gloom behind bars.

12th December 1965

МОЛИТВА

Я охвачен тихой паникой,
Я вступаю с богом в торги,
Наперед обещаю быть паинькой
И шепчу ему: "Помоги!"

Обещаю грешить не часто,
Пить по малу и спать с одной —
"Отгони от меня несчастье,
Схорони за своей спиной.

Теплым ветром ударь об окна
И вручи мне незримый щит."
Я молю о защите, а бог-то —
Он ведь тоже не лыком шит.

Вспоминает он доскональный
Всю мою непутевую жизнь.
И в ответ громыхает: "Каналья.
Не кощунствуй и не божись."

Видно знает вернее, чем следствие,
Что меня не отмыть до бела,
Что навряд ли придут в соответствие
Обещанья мои и дела.

30.I2.65

A PRAYER

I am possessed by silent panic,
I am beginning to haggle with God.
I promise him to be a good boy in future
And I whisper to him: "Help me!"

    I promise to sin less frequently,
    To drink in moderation, to sleep with one girl.
    "Please avert the catastrophe,
    Hide me behind your back."

"Beat at the windows like a warm wind,
Grant me an invisible shield!"
I crave His protection, but God
Just isn't that much of a fool.

    He remembers in detail
    The whole of my backsliding life.
    And He thunders in answer: "You, wretch,
    Do not blaspheme, do not take my name in vain!"

He probably knows better than my interrogators
That I can never be washed white,
That my promises and actions
Aren't ever likely to agree.

30th December 1965

НОВОГОДНИЙ МАРШ—ДЕКЛАРАЦИЯ

Когда вверх тормашками катится
И бьется в падучей судьба,
Не надо молиться и каяться,
Бояться сумы и суда.

Оглядывай пристальней прошлое
Без лести оценивай дни,
Окурки иллюзий – подошвою.
А светлому – грудь распахни:

Не сдайся бессилью и горечи,
Не дайся неверью и лжи –
Не все лизоблюды и сволочи,
Не все стукачи и ханжи.

Шагая дорогами чуждыми
В какой-то неведомый край,
Друзей имена, как жемчужины,
Как четки перебирай.

Будь зорким, веселым и яростным
И выстоишь, выстоишь ты
Под грузом невзгод многоярусных,
Под ношей своей правоты.

31.12.65

THE NEW YEAR MARCH: A DECLARATION

When your life is tumbling downhill head over heels,
Thrashing and foaming like an epileptic,
Don't pray and offer up repentance,
Don't be afraid of jail and ruin.

Study your past with concentration,
Evaluate your days without self-flattery,
Grind the fag-ends of illusions underfoot,
But open up to all that's bright and clear.

Don't surrender to impotence and bitterness,
Don't give in to disbelief and lies,
Not everyone's a cringing bastard,
Not everyone's a bigot who informs.

And while you walk along the alien roads
To lands which do not figure on your maps,
Count out the names of all your friends
As you would do with pearls or prayer-beads.

Be on the look-out, cheerful and ferocious,
And you'll manage to stand up, yes, stand up
Under your many-layered load of misery,
Under the burden of your being right.

31st December 1965

А вдруг вот так приходит зрелость,
Когда впотьмах спасенья ищем:
"Мне автором прослыть хотелось" –
Твердит испуганный Радищев.

Когда на торную дорогу
Впотьмах бредем, себя жалея:
"Земля недвижна ... Грешен Богу ..."
Петляет голос Галилея.

А вдруг вот так приходит смелость –
Хитрить, не труся непочета:
Ведь то, что как-то раз пропелось,
Уже не спишется со счета.

А вдруг разумна Божья милость:
Мы все в ничто пустое канем,
И то, что как-то воплотилось,
Не зачеркнется покаяньем.

... Но, вспоминая в час вечерний
Про все про то, что днем сказали,
Как жить нам после отречений?
Какими нам истечь слезами ?

"A better victory, perhaps..."
                                Marina Tsvetayeva

"I've grown wise..."
                                Alexander Pushkin

"I wanted to be thought of as an author,"
The frightened Radishchev kept repeating -
Who knows? This may be how maturity begins
When we are groping for salvation in the dark.

"The earth is motionless...I've sinned before God..."
The voice of Galileo went on mumbling,
As we wandered onto the highway
Out of the darkness, sorry for ourselves.

Who knows? Perhaps this is the birth of courage -
Use cunning, don't be fearful of disgrace,
For once your singing has become your song
It can't go traceless like a thing unsung.

Who knows? God's grace may still be rational:
We shall all disappear into the void,
But what has taken on an actual shape
Will not be cancelled out by mere repentance.

...But now filled with recollection in the dusk
Of all we spoke of in the daylight hours,
With our beliefs discarded, how can we live?
What shall we use for tears to drain our eyes?

Что думать жесткими ночами
О сбереженной нашей жизни,
Когда герои за плечами
В немой застыли укоризне? ..

5.I.66

What shall we think during the hard nights
About our lives salvaged from wrecks?
When heroes looming up behind
Are turned to ice, reproaching silently?

5th January 1966

1965 ГОД

А что мне с вашей томной негой,
Когда от бешеной тоски:
— Дружок мой, за бутылкой сбегай,
Омоем новые носки.

А что мне ваши ахи, охи,
Рулады светских Лорелей?
— Дела, дружок мой, очень плохи,
А ну-ка новую налей.

Я бесконечным ожиданьем,
Как труп щетиною оброс ...
— Давай еще одну раздавим,
Омоем пачку папирос.

Моей тоске еврейско-русской
Сродни и водка, и кровать ...
— Да хрен с ней, с этою закуской,
Пора остатки допивать.

Пора допить остатки смеха,
Допить измены, страсть и труд.
— Хана, дружок мой. Я приехал,
Пускай войдут и заберут.

10.I.66

1965

I don't give a damn for your sweet feelings of bliss.
I'm sick at heart, the only cure is if you say:
"Run out, my friend, and buy a bottle,
We'll drink a toast to a new pair of socks."

Don't give a damn for your "ahs" and "ohs",
Or even the trilling of modish Loreleis.
"Listen my friend, I'm lower than low,
Just pour me another."

I am overgrown with endless waiting
Like a corpse with a beard that keeps growing from
    stubble.
"Let's crack another bottle -
To a fresh packet of cigarettes."

My Jewish-Russian mortal anguish
Takes to the vodka and then to bed.
"Who wants chasers?
It's time to drain the dregs."

It's time to drain the dregs of laughter,
To swallow infidelities, passion and work.
"It's all over, my friend, I've come home.
Let them come in and take me away."

10th January 1966

Дожди, дожди коснулись щек,
Грустя, деревья порыжели,
И был открыт несчастный счет
Моих побед и поражений.

Струилась осень, день за днем
Линяла летняя палитра,
А я во всю играл с огнем
И тайно жаждал опалиться.
Не потому, что я, шальной,
Роптал перед глухой стеною —
Я преступил закон иной,
Я виноват иной виною.

И не за то, что я кричал,
Меня, сойдясь, осудят судьи —
За то, что на свою печаль,
Как пластырь клал чужие судьбы.

За то, что я , сойдя с ума,
Не пощадил чужого сердца,
А суд, законы и тюрьма —
Всего лишь кнут, всего лишь средство,
Возмездие за тайный грех,
За то, что, убивая, выжил ...
И вот зима.   И страшен снег,
Запятнанный капелью рыжей.

13.I.66

Raindrops, raindrops touched my cheeks,
The trees turned fiery red from sorrow,
And the miserable account lay open,
Record of my victories and defeats.

Autumn was under way. Day after day
Summer's palette was fading,
While I played for excessive stakes with fire
And getting my fingers burned was my secret wish.
Wishing for it not because in my delusion
I grumbled that the wall was blind.
I broke a different sort of law,
My guilt was of a different kind.

Judges in consultation will condemn me
Not for speaking out too loud,
But for tearing bandages for my sorrows
Out of other people's lives.

For my unwillingness to spare another's heart
In my insanity.
And as for courts, and law, and prison,
They're no more than a whip, a means towards an end.
The retribution for a secret sin,
My own survival while I made others die.
Now winter's here. The snow is frightening
Where it lies melted into stains as red as fire.

13th January 1966

59

НА РИНГЕ

Я вышел, боксом не владея,
Рискнув удачливой судьбой.
Не звал ни бога, ни людей я –
И проиграл до боя бой.

Толпа – грохочущая прорва,
Перчатки – парою гранат.
Удар. Я смят, отброшен, взорван.
И спину мне обжег канат.

Удар. Бесстрастно смотрят судьи,
Как дышит голая душа,
Как до моей, до голой сути
Добрался мастер не спеша.

Он – бог. Его движенья четки,
Как протоколы – без прикрас.
И ставят черные перчатки
Удары – точки после фраз.

Мне от беды не отвертеться,
Меня везде достанет плеть;
А все ж не будет полотенца
У ног, постыдное, белеть.

Я жду: сейчас меня накажут
За дерзость и за простоту.
Ну что же – бой. Пускай нокаут
Под схваткой подведет черту.

IN THE RING

I came into the ring, and not a boxer
My chances were pinned onto my lucky stars.
Invoking neither God nor populace
I lost the fight before it had begun.

The crowd is like a thundering precipice,
The gloves are like a pair of hand grenades.
A punch! I'm crushed, repulsed, exploded,
The searing rope now burns into my back.

A punch! The referees watch quite unperturbed
The way a soul stripped bare is breathing.
The way the champion got straight to my naked essence
In his own unhurried fashion.

He is a Deity. His movements are precise.
Like reams of evidence - without embellishment.
His black gloves punctuate with blows
Like full stops at the ends of sentences.

There is no way for me to dodge this trouble,
The whip will find me everywhere.
And yet the white towel of cowardice
Will not be thrown into the ring.

I am now waiting to be punished
For my defiance, for my simplicity.
All right, let's fight! Let the knockout
Reckon up the total of the match.

Я поражение любое
Приму, зажав губами крик.
Не для победы, а для боя
Я шел на ринг.

16.I.66

I'll accept any defeat that's handed me,
Smother my groans behind my tight-closed lips.
It was not to win but fight
That I came into the ring.

16th January 1966

И ЕЩЕ О ДРУЗЬЯХ

Мы выстроились все в одну шеренгу,
Готовые к походу и параду.
- На правом фланге. Застегни ширинку.
- На левом фланге. Оботри помаду.

Друг друга мы, любя, глазами ели,
Глядели браво, преданно и гордо.
И я подумал, что на самом деле
Мы все - непобедимая когорта.

Идет начальство, шествуя вдоль строя,
И все, казалось, было б тихо-мирно,
Да вот беда: из строя вышли трое
И доносили, встав по стойке "смирно".

Товарищ наш , - они сказали, - бяка.
Он-вольнодум, он - враг верховной воли.
Он кашу ест, как все мы, но однако,
Он говорит, что в каше мало соли.

И весь парад накрылся в одночасье.
Сказали мне: "В семье не быть уроду."
Я получил по шее от начальства
И послан был в штрафную роту.

26.I.66

MORE ABOUT MY FRIENDS

We were all standing in a single line
Ready for parade and for taking the field.
"Hey, you on the left! See to your flies!"
"Hey, you on the right! Wipe the lipstick off your
    face!"

We loved each other, were always looking at each other
We seemed so proud, so dashing and devoted.
For a moment I believed that we
All belonged to an insuperable band.

The officers came striding down the line,
To me it all seemed very peaceful -
Then the first sign of trouble: three men stepped out
And, standing to attention, made their report.

Our friend, they said, has been quite naughty.
He's a free-thinker, he's hostile to authority,
He eats his porridge, the same as we do, but he likes
Insisting that it's not been properly salted.

The whole parade was scattered in a second,
"The black sheep will be thrown out" I was told.
I got it in the neck from my non-com
And was pushed off to the punishment brigade.

26th January 1966

РОМАНС О РОДИНЕ

Страна моя, скажи мне хоть словечко.
Перед тобой душа моя чиста.
Неужто так, бесстыдно и навечно
Тебя со мной разделит клевета?

Свои мечты сбивая в кровь о камни,
Я шел к тебе сквозь жар и холода,
Я шел с тобой. Я шел, и на глаза мне,
Как слезы, наплывали города.

Я не таю ни помысла дурного,
Ни сожалений о своей судьбе,
Страна моя, ну вымолви хоть слово,
Ведь знаешь ты, что я не лгал тебе.

Ведь не бросал влюбленность на весы я
И страсть мою на доли не дробил —
Я так любил тебя, моя Россия,
Как, может быть, и женщин не любил.

Чтоб никогда не сетовал на долю,
Чтоб не упал под тяжестью креста,
Страна моя, коснись меня ладонью —
Перед тобой душа моя чиста.

29.I.66

A LOVE SONG ABOUT MY COUNTRY

My country, all I want from you is one small word!
My soul before you is unblemished.
Can slander really stand between you and me -
Like this, shamelessly and for ever?

Wearing my dreams away on your stones until I bled,
I marched to you through heat and cold.
I marched with you. I marched, and your cities
Welled up into my eyes like tears.

I have no bad intentions,
Not even regrets about my fate.
My country, please just say a word,
You know I never lied to you.

I never flung my love for you onto the scales
Or tried to portion out my passion.
I loved you so much, my Russia,
Even more, perhaps, than I loved women.

So that my fate should never give me grief,
So that I should never bow under a heavy cross,
Touch me with your palm, my country -
My soul before you is unblemished.

29th January 1966

ОБВИНИТЕЛЬНОЕ ЗАКЛЮЧЕНИЕ

(краткий конспект)

К словесности влеченье
Нуждается в леченьи –
Ведь все без исключенья
Тлетворны увлеченья.

Умозаключение:
"Тела заключение".

5.2.66

THE INDICTMENT

(a summary)

An attraction to literature
Requires a proper cure.
It is a ruinous temptation
As are all temptations.

"Remand the man in custody",
This judgement is a Q.E.D.

5th February 1966

ПРО ЭТИ СТИХИ

Мои стихи — как пасмурные дни,
В них нету зноя.
Совсем не мной написаны они,
А может,мною ?

Они грустят у запертых дверей,
У синих коек.
И пафос их не стоит лагерей,
А может,стоит ?

Им не уйти, не скрыться нипочем
От этих буден.
Их петь не будет Лешка Пугачев,
А может, будет?

Им не прорвать, не смять железный круг,
Их уничтожат,
Их прочитать не сможет милый друг,
А может, сможет?

Они в ночи не принесут врагам
Зубовный скрежет.
И подлецам не врежут по мозгам,
А может, врежут?

17.2.66

ABOUT THESE POEMS

My poems are like days all clouded over,
Untouched by the hot sun.
It wasn't really me who made them.
Or was it?

Immersed in gloom they stand beside locked doors,
Beside blue-covered bunks.
Their passion isn't worth my going to the camps.
Or is it?

They can't release themselves, they won't escape
From this tormented life.
Lyoshka Pugachyov won't sing them.
Or will he?

They'll never crack the iron ring, never smash through
    it,
They'll be obliterated.
A loving friend will never read them.
Or will he?

At night they'll never force my enemies
To grind their teeth.
Nor will they strike the bastards dumb.
Or will they?

17th February 1966

ПРИГОВОР

Да не посмеешь думать о своем,
Вздыхать о доме и гнушаться пищей,
Ты — объектив, ты — лист бумаги писчей,
Ты брошен сетью в этот водоем.

Чужие скорби грусть твоя вберет,
Умножит годы лагерная старость,
И лягут грузом на твою усталость
Чужие строки северных широт.

Пускай твоя саднящая мозоль
Напоминает о чужих увечьях.
Ты захлебнулся в судьбах человечьих,
Твоей судьбой отныне будет боль.

И будешь ты вседневно грань стирать
Меж легким "я" и многотонным "все мы",
И за других, чьи смерти были немы,
И будешь ты вседневно умирать.

И будет солона твоя вода
И горек хлеб, и сны не будут сниться,
Пока вокруг ты видишь эти лица,
И в черных робах мается беда.

. . . .

Приговору отвечаю: ДА.

22.2.66

72

THE SENTENCE

You will not dare to think your own thoughts,
Sigh for home or refuse to eat the food.
You are a lens, you are a blank sheet of paper,
You are cast into this water like a net.

Your sadness will absorb all alien sadness,
Prison will prolong your years into old age,
And wearying you will have to bear a burden -
The lines of unfamiliar northern latitudes.

May your smarting callouses
Remind you of others being mutilated.
You are submerged in human destiny,
From now on your destiny is pain.

Every day you will rub out the line
Dividing the weightless "I" from the massive "All".
Every day you will die a death for others
Who died mute deaths.

Your water will be brine
Your bread will be bitter and you will have no dreams
As long as you see these faces about you,
As long as prisoners in black suffer in wretchedness.

. . . .

Do I accept my sentence? Yes, I do.

22nd February 1966

ФЕВРАЛЬ

А за окном такая благодать,
Такое небо – детское, весеннее,
Что, кажется, мне незачем и ждать
Другого утешенья и спасения.

Забыто зло, которое вчера
Горланило и души нам коверкало.
Ну, милые, ну, женщины, пора
Взглянуть в окно, как вы глядите в
    зеркало.

Уже плывет снегов седая шерсть,
И за окном, как серьги, виснут каплищи.
Еще чуть-чуть – и всем вам хорошеть,
Сиять глазам, платкам спускаться
    на плечи.

Еще чуть-чуть– и вам ночей не спать,
Мечтать взахлеб и все дела откладывать,
На улице года помчаться вспять,
И у прохожих будет дух захватывать.

(А в этот миг умолкнет перестук,
Собрав мешок, на перестанке выйду я,
За тыщу верст учую красоту
И улыбнусь, ревнуя и завидуя).

И вас весна до самого нутра
Проймет словами – нежными и грубыми.
Ну, милые, – пора, пора,
Расстаться вам с печалями и с шубами.

                        22.2.66

FEBRUARY

Outside my window the day is radiant
The sky shows spring and is child-painted blue;
It seems I have no reason to expect
Comfort or hope of help apart from this.

Evil is quite forgotten. Only yesterday
It howled and crucified our souls.
And so, dear girls, and so it's time for me
To look through the window as you would look into a
    mirror.

Now the grey wool of the snow is unravelled
And outside the window great drops dangle like ear-rings.
A few more days and you'll all be prettier
With shining eyes and kerchiefs round your shoulders.

A few more days, then no more sleep at night,
You'll dream uncurbed, put off your daily tasks.
Outside, the years will rush into reverse
Drawing the breath away from everyone.

(And then the clatter of the wheels will stop,
I'll pack my satchel and get off at a tiny station.
I'll scent the beauty a thousand miles away,
And then I'll smile all envious and grudging.)

The spring will pierce you through and through
With its words, coarse ones as well as tender.
Well, dear girls, it's time, it's really time
For you to shed your sorrows and your furs.

22nd February 1966

NOTES ON THE POEMS

Page 21, line 2. January was the date originally set
for Daniel's trial, but it was later postponed until
February.

Page 31, line 2. F. Panfyorov's novel about
collectivization, The Whetstones, is typical of
orthodox fiction - the only fiction available in
prison libraries.

Page 43, line 12. The "dark and terrible three years"
were the years during which Daniel was publishing
his prose in the West under the pseudonym of
"Nikolai Arzhak" and managing to keep this a
secret from the Soviet authorities.

Page 53, epigraph. Marina Tsvetayeva (1894-1941) is
one of the great tragic and romantic poets of
modern Russia. The epigraph is an allusion to her
suicide.

Page 53, line 2. Radishchev, who lived in the
eighteenth century, was the first Russian
revolutionary writer. When his book A Journey
from Petersburg to Moscow was published,
shortly after the French Revolution, it was
noticed by the Empress Catherine and branded
as subversive. The author was sentenced to
death, but repented and was exiled instead.

Page 71, line 11. Lyoshka Pugachyov is well known
for his recitative verse singing accompanied by a
guitar.